from
Adina Cherkin
She died on
Tuesday November 11th
The memorial celebration
was on Nov 15th/14
at Kingsleymanor

TERSE VERSE

&

Oodles of Doodles

by

Adina Cherkin

DORRANCE PUBLISHING CO., INC.
PITTSBURGH, PENNSYLVANIA 15222

ISBN # 0-8059-4894-5
Printed in the United States of America

First Printing

For information or to order additional books, please write:
Dorrance Publishing Co., Inc.
643 Smithfield Street
Pittsburgh, Pennsylvania 15222
U.S.A.
1-800-788-7654

Lovingly,

to all the delightful derelicts

who have made my life

meaningful.

A. C.

Table of Contents

Introduction .... ix–xiii

A Sampling of Readers' Comments xv

About the Author .... xvii–xxi

OF WESTERN HAIKUS, MONGRELS, AND OTHER BLASTARDS

Magician 3

Splish 5

Auto 7

Willy 9

Swish 11

Ping! (1) 13

Quality Beer 15

Seamstress 17

Lose Tickee? 19

Ping (2) 21

Top 23

Teacher 25

Happiness 27

Peter Patrick 29

Sultans 31

Mopey Dick 33

Skeletons 35

Bose 37

Muse 39

George 41

Whirling 43

Chill 45

Golly Leo 47

No Longer 49

PUBLISHED POETRY (First Rights Only)

Ungrateful Patient 53
  The Journal of Irreproducible Results

De Transplantibus Disputandum 55
  The Journal of Biological Psychology / The Worm Runner's Digest

A Chrissinning Which Lost its "T" in the Gulf Coarse 57
  New Voices

Reflections on Seymour Benzer's Fly Paper 59
  Caltech Biology Annual

Annass 61
  The California Tech, California Institute of Technology

Parthenogenesis 63
  The Journal of Biological Psychology / The Worm Runner's Digest

LONG POEMS – SENTIMENTAL POETRY – IMAGERY

Painful Crimson 67

Whose Kudos? 69

Why Purr? 71

Gentlemen's Agleement 73

Wednesday 75

The Mistress 77–81

Amsteldrama 83

Who the Hell is Mary-Lu? 85–87

Horse Around 89

Solitude à Deux 91

A Stitch in Time 93

Glorious Doll 95

Fugglegudgets 97

Slippery Dick 99–101

A Knight on the King'th Mount 103

Borderline 105

DITTIES

Confusion 109

Whoa! 111

Addiction 113

Eve'n Steven 115

Of Slobber-Drewly Dogs 117

Nestling Urge 119

On the Verge of Liberation 121

I Wonder Why 123

My Mother Says 125

Hell, You Can Tell 127

As the Saying Goes 129

Shellfish He-gloatist 131

Cockteaser's Professed Credo 133

After Beast Turns Panting Beauty Down 135

FOREIGN POETRY – ACROSTICS

Full Circle 139

Eulogy 141

Confessions de "Linguiste?" 142–143

Peace 145

Jonah 147

To a Friend? 149

Summer 1985 151

Frommage! 153

To E. W. 155

Of Pipes and Ventilation 157

Confession Matinale 158–159

Trilogy: 160–163
    I. Over an Overstoughed Russian Final
    II. Overstoughed Russian Final
    III. Over a Russian Final - A Redress

Macaronics 165

ONE-LETTER AND PUNCTUATION POEMS

The Purpose of My Life 169

You & Thou 171

Besieging 173

Before the "Final Period" 175

Lovers' Lost Week-end 177

After a Tryst 179

Regimentation with a Tail 181

My One and Only Friend 182–183

Gemini 184–185

Cri du Coeur 186–187

About "The Story of O!" 188–189

Mort aux Poissons 190–191

G.M.B.H. 192–193

Birth of a Spanish Coryza 194–195

The Birth of a Cold 196–197

Double Gemini 198–199

In Two Stanzas 200–201

Cadeau de Bourreau 202–203

PROFESSIONAL ODDBALLS

T.V. Executives 207

To My Lawyer 209

Surgeon Talk 211

Plastic Diagnostic 213

To My Disjointed Lawyer 215

ILLUSTRATIVE POEMS

O Yes Guilt 219

Ectoplasm 221

Which Carroll? 223

August 1987 225

The Empty Glass 227

Respect 229

A.C. 230–231

Introduction

Amusing as it may be,

For me,

The Muse is definitely a HE.

Curious to test readers' acceptance of a manuscript that does not fit the general pattern, I shared it with a wide spectrum of readers. From seniors to an eleven-year-old granddaughter, from university professors to high school graduates, from enthusiasts to sour pusses — the consensus, enthusiastic without exception, was that it indeed deserved publication. Invariably they queried how I had come to conceive and give birth to such a whimsical baby. How long had been the gestation period? Who was the father ... or was it in-vitro fertilization?

To my surprise, after hearing my answer, they generally suggested that I include the following in my introduction:

For over 20 years I have gone through periodic surges of "creative" writing — mostly poetry. I would usually wake up suddenly in the dark of night. The surges engendered urges to commit to paper, pell-mell and uncensored, whatever words and thoughts surfaced. The next morning, in utter amazement, I would find notes with kooky ideas, which I did not recognize as coming from me. To be candid, at times I was a bit scared of that uninvited tenant within me... However, as we became better acquainted, I started to enjoy and appreciate his presence and we became lovers. Thus were born various genres of poems — long and short, sentimental and satirical, serious and humorous, English and multilingual, haikus, ditties, acrostics and even "one-letter poems". In all, over 120 of them... For years I would file them away and forget they existed.

In parallel and totally unconnected with the above, I managed to collect close to 650 sketches. They were penned or penciled hastily at conferences and lectures when my hands refused to remain inactive. Thus came to life portraits, caricatures, men, women and children, animal scenes, plant and sea life, monsters and fairies,

rubbish and garbage. These sketches revealed to me a great deal about my inner-self. Again I was in awe at the previously unrecognized life that populated my depths and I grew more and more eager to bring it out into the light.

After leading a creative double life for over two decades, one day it occurred to me to unite the two forms in marriage. I spread the sketches by categories on my dining room table (open to banquet size!), on my two buffets and on several folding tables. Then, with one poem in hand at a time, I "shopped around" until I made a match. To my exhilaration, I was able to pair off every single poem in a jiffy. Not a single bachelor was left stranded!

The next step, the most laborious, yet so enjoyable, entailed the *"mise-en-page"*: harmonious presentation of the newlyweds within one-inch margins, selection of appropriate fonts for maximum "atmosphere," reduction or enlargement, deletions or additions, plus a balancing of hormones to allow satisfying consummation of the marriage and ensure enduring vitality of the union.

In brief, my mood throughout the book's more-than-two-years of gestation can best be described as *"three-dimensional orgasmic enjoyment"*.

How personable is the offspring? ... That remains for *you* to decide.

A.C.

My heartfelt gratitude to Betsy Hall for her enthusiastic collaboration in preparing the manuscript. Betsy's dedication to detail went beyond the call of duty. Without her this book would not have been published. My thanks also go to Maureen Brogan for her great support and for her shared knowledge of the publishing field.

A Sampling of Readers' Comments

"Your poems were so good that we found room for them in the next issue. We will be absolutely delighted to receive future contributions from you."

Nancy Crockett, Managing Editor
The Journal of Biological Psychology, The University of Michigan Press

"I was delighted to receive the antidote [collection of poems]. It worked. I was absoluterly abfloundered and demused."

James L. McGaugh, Professor of Psychology
University of California, Riverside

"Adina is a wizard (or witch?) with language."

Edwin Honig, Poet-Scholar
(as quoted by Victor Terras, Professor of Slavic Languages, Brown University)

"We arrived back from Mexico City and to our utter happiness had your delightful letter and poetry. Fatigued as we were (seventeen hours on the trip home) we sat down and laughed and laughed over the delightful absurdities and penetration."

Seymour M. Farber, MD, Vice Chancellor
University of California, San Francisco

"During my thirty-two years working with Walt Disney, I saw many attempts by writers to create new styles and unusual uses of words with illustrations, but none of them appealed to me as much as these poems of yours.... There is a fresh, lilting quality in these writings, and the matching drawings have created a treasured concept.... The whimsy, the wit, the charm and the provocative philosophy will at last be available to sophisticates wherever they may be."

Frank Thomas, Animation Director
Walt Disney Studios

About the Author

me

I'm not a young chick anymore ...

But I swirl, and I dance,

And I fence ... with words!

And I marvel at the birds.

And I enjoy helping others,

Be they fathers or mothers.

I'm compassionate ... but not weak!

Five languages I fluently speak.

I love to write, and I doodle ...

So, you see, I'm not quite a noodle.

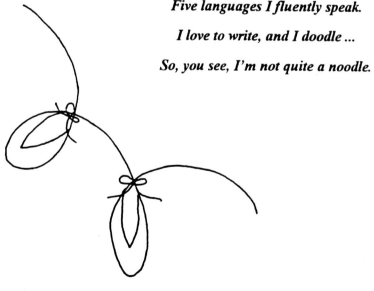

Adina Mantchik Cherkin has had a checkered career.

Born of Russian parents in Geneva, Switzerland, she prepared herself at an early age to study Medicine… to be like her father. As an adolescent, she also trained in ballet and drama, and appeared in acting and dancing parts on the Geneva stage.

In 1940 she emigrated to the United States with her family. Two years later, after having completed her pre-medical studies at UCLA, she was recommended by Governor Olson of California to Secretary of State Cordell Hull to work as a censor in Washington DC. On January 3, 1942 she was invited by the Roosevelts to have dinner at the White House. Eleanor Roosevelt then referred her to several government heads for eventual positions in Washington. Her naturalization process was accelerated to make her eligible to work in the US Government.

After all the commotion, she declined the various job offers and gave up as well her studies to become a doctor. Instead, she married Arthur Cherkin, a biochemist in the pharmaceutical field. They had two children, Della and Daniel, and five grandchildren. While raising her family, Adina acted as interpreter in French, English, German, and Russian for Baxter Laboratories, Walt Disney Studios, the US Immigration and Naturalization Service and as a science translator for UCLA Medical School. She occasionally took up acting, and appeared on NBC with Charles Boyer in "A Date with Judy." In her spare time Adina worked for the campaigns of California Supreme Court Judge Stanley Mosk and California State Senator Alan Cranston.

After her children left the nest, Adina returned to UCLA where she earned both B.A. and M.A. degrees in Russian Linguistics and Literature. She then worked several years with manuscripts and artwork by well-known Russian writers and artists — a collection inherited from members of her family. She investigated universities and museums in Russia and Europe, eventually placing these valuable works in proper "homes."

In 1973, after her father's passing, Adina took over his leadership of the Herz Mantchik Amity Circle, a cultural forum for Jewish studies. It subsequently earned her a Los Angeles City Council "Award for Contributions to the Community."

For the next twenty-five years Adina devoted more and more of her time to Jewish causes. On occasion she also acted as advisor to several Christian Zionist leaders. Her interests in Russian studies and Jewish causes extended to helping Russian Jews who came to Los Angeles as immigrants and students. In 1993 she funded a Chair in Food Engineering at Israel's Technion Institute of Technology.

One of Adina's success stories was overcoming a serious bout with cancer. In 1992 she was diagnosed with an advanced stage of "lethal" colon malignancy. After an initial surgery, Adina refused the toxic chemotherapy her oncologist deemed essential to her survival. She spent over a month thoroughly researching alternative treatments, and embarked on a course of immune system enhancement. This enabled her strengthened body to take over and fight off the disease. For the next five years she had no recurrence and was declared cancer-free.

Some of Adina's poetry, mostly medical satire, has been published at the California Institute of Technology, University of Michigan Press, and others. *Terse Verse & Oodles of Doodles* is her first book.

Of

Western Haikus,

Mongrels,

and Other

Blastards

𝔐agician
Jailed.

Illegal
to
Harbor cadaber.

Splish in pond!

~~Ripple~~

...Hook splash...

Fish dish!

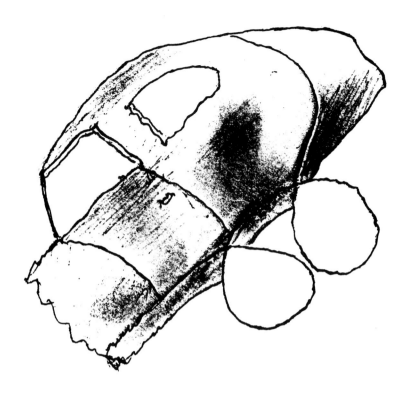

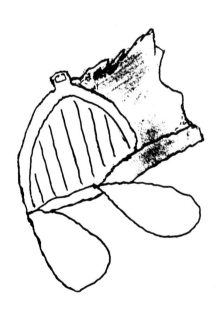

Auto

misses

curve.

Topsy-curvy . . .

Autopsy!

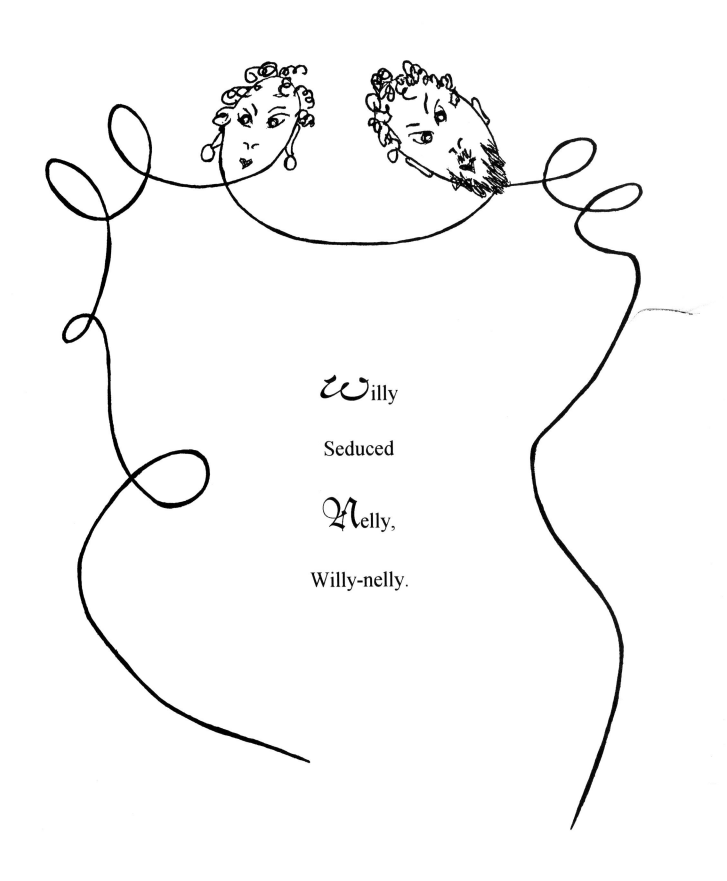

Willy

Seduced

Nelly,

Willy-nelly.

Swish!

Blue wife

in

Yellow kimono

Rush by,

Green...

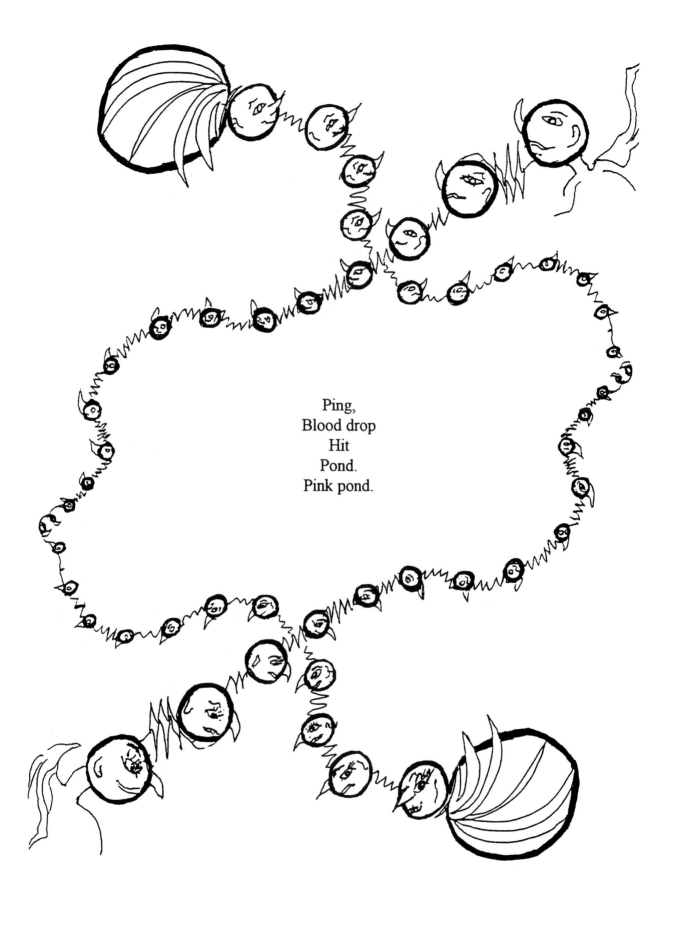

Ping,
Blood drop
Hit
Pond.
Pink pond.

Quality

beer

made

here,

Hippety hops!

Seamstress

a

Spinster

She

does

Sew-so

Lose
Tickee?
So sorry
you
Wishee washee!

Ping!
Rain drops
Hit
Pond
Ping pond.

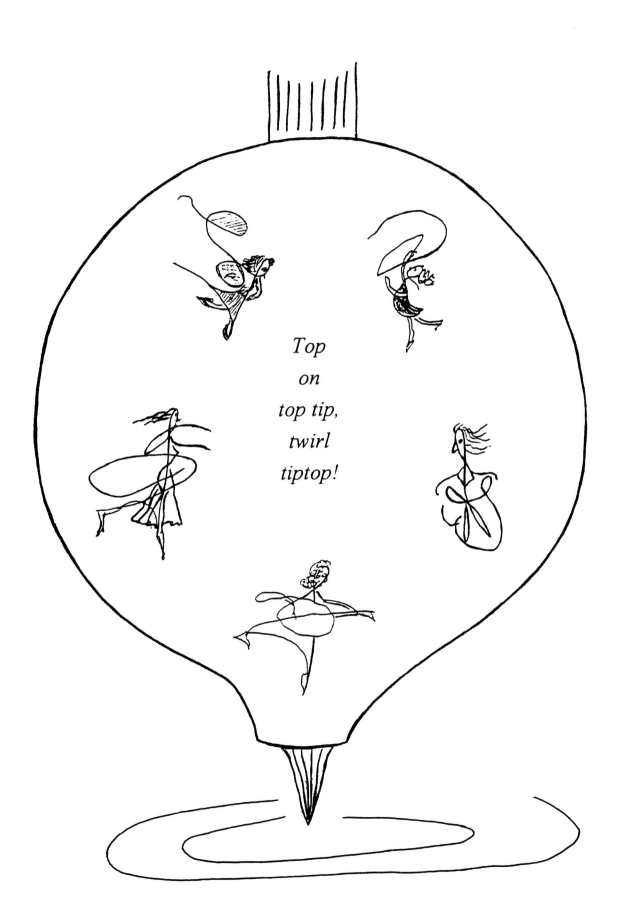

Top
on
top tip,
twirl
tiptop!

Teacher

Angry.

Spank

Hank.

Hanky-spanky!

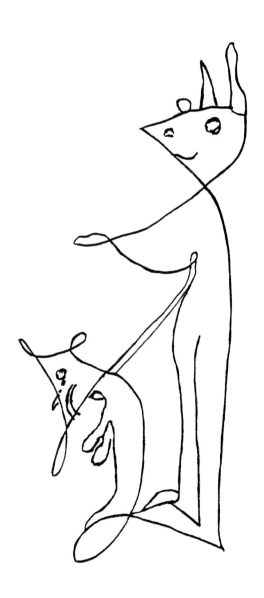

Happiness is

not hearing
"Happiness is . . ."

Little Peter Patrick,

So Sick,

Soon . . .

No Pitter-Patterick!

Mopey Dick
is
a whale of
a
sad prick

SKELETONS
IN
HELL,
HELLTER-SKELLETER

Bose Blocked.

Allergy...

Not Fuddy, Daddy!

Muse,

Dilly Dali

in Museum

Gallely!

GEORGE
GORGED

BANANA,
ICE CREAM,

LICKETY-
SPLIT

Whirling dervish's

Preemie

Named:

"Too early"

Chill

on

Chin...

no

Chinchilla!

No

Chill

on

Chin...

Chinchilla!

Golly, Leo!

You

No

Study

Galileo?

*...No longer
can I
afford
the afore-mentioned
mansion...*

Published Poetry

Ungrateful

Patient

M edical science has prodigressed . . . much beyond the horse and bogey.
E ntraptured with being processed . . . from young 'n hale to lame 'n fogey
L eap'n heap in increasing number . . . for mult-stetho-retino-proctoscopy
A uscultations, punctions lumbar . . . RBC and EEG, or cardiac horoscopy.
N e'er having cared to be outdone . . . throngs I joined at the internist...
O grim his referral up an echelon! . . . Grimmer the vow o' the gynecologist:
" M elanom—(Hmm!)—pigmentation . . . exfoliation? . . . Blackspot — biopsy!"
" A h, Doctor, heed my imploration . . . Save me! Shall there by an autopsy?"

Sutures six in my engina non-pectoris:
Stinguin sanguin penguin ploddle.
Sutures six in my arsenal non-rectalis:
Ducky wacky walking woddle.

M any 'n long the minute, the hours . . . Musn't tell hedon-hubby, no-ways!
E xacting taxing nights of horror . . . Till the verdict — four more days...
L onesome, oh alone-so-me-mories: . . . Sweet life's past, with no future.
A fter insomnia — biomed-libraries . . . (Sit softly, don't pop a suture!)
N o dearth in lit on black pigment . . . Alas all with prognosis no-roses!
O rder in my affairs. A testament . . . Then seconambiturate overdoses...
...M onday at last! Phoned verdict from Above: malignancy none, but a freckle
" A plain old freckle? Heckle! And for *this* you wreckled me, Jekyll!"

DE TRANSPLANTIBUS DISPUTANDUM

From Johannesiceberg to Siam
Dr. Barnard, Christ-i-am,
Has launched with nervrogance impetulous
The Transplant Age stimultuous.
Each Tom, Mick de Bakey, and Harry
On the band wagging jumps
From Blaiberg's bod to Barry's
To transshift lumps.
Jiggling eyeballs, rognons, tickers,
Milts, wombs, rockmount'n oysters,
To man they bring metampsorphosis
With multiple scloriginosis.
Remiss below the neckline to remain
And aiming for the climapex supreme,
Their fingers, on the greedeager beam,
Already reach to leech the brain.
They say soon problems of rejection
Will cease to avoid detection
And Sis Brown's brain'll be transplanted
Into Methuselah Smith's body.
This is, meseems, doddy-shoddy;
For, in truth, Mathuselah Smith's body
To Sis Brown's brain shall be transplanted.

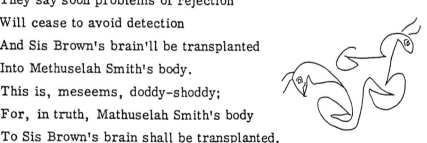

A CHRISSINNING WHICH LOST ITS 'T' IN THE GULF COARSE

The hour sex, the day was night.
Debauched she sat under the light.
The climate warm. Her mood was fresh
Which from her sill proposed her flesh.

'long the canal strolled he and I.
I caught her catch my husband's eye.
Her hands cupping her cantaliver,
Bouncerósly promised to deliver
That which the skinny me could not.
Remember us, her eyes suggested,
Caressing his culotte;
Upon her breasts they rested;
Forget-us-not. Forget-us-not . . .

Hubby surveyed her naked acreage
Which doubly flowed to wom'ly cleaverage
And where already lay,
As if to point the way,
A diamond-studded crossifix.

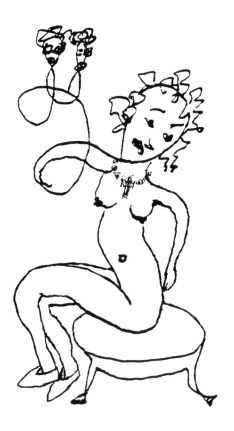

New Voices in American Poetry
1972, page 151 • Vantage Press, Inc.

Reflections on
Seymour Benzer's Fly Paper:
"From the Gene to Behavior"

T hen operation Big Bang geneticists blastulated — Grigorous Mendel first eclose **D**

H is immutant penchant for longshortstem sweetpeas, of Red-Cross blooms made him fathe **R**

O rganisms galore (rotedervishers, paradigmecia, mnematodes, Escherichia colonic, phyc **O**

M yces and mices) in biochem – ana *tom* ical searches more & morecular, in coding **S**

A nd structures were used, for philo- and ontogene- antics with nevarious degrees **O'**

S excess … Caltech "chromato" selected my left acrostician to put me right on the ma **P**

H e & his breed with tlecherous mutagens my urgenitors *hunt* ed — never heard'm cry ouc **H!**

U nder strained, subcoding conditions he kept 'm, invoking a neuronicly - linked alib **I,**

N ormal behavior for Homo Sapiens!… Little did we know that our trial was trivia **L**

T il Zer begat Seymour.   Then why plus sex begat to fly! . . . I metamorphomosaic-ed in **A**

M énage *morgan* atic: my melanopater ethyl-methane-subformated, mom with no savoir-rhyth **M**

O h what freaks abound me! Slugalong, Grounded, Eggdropper, Twins-in-onebody … I ask yo **U!**

R ut-time for Stuck, for Drop-dead, for cuz'n who thinks he knows how when he doesn' **T**

G rave missery did prove — all for the voyerg ratification of a night owl's generotic **A!**

A vec this super - energenetic, sex - demoniac ("fun" he calls it!) S. B. predestinaria **N**

N o blim'd prefractionized drosophilhombre can ever betrussed to keep his fly shu **T!**

Thomas Hunt Morgan (1866 – 1945): Geneticist, 1933 Nobel prize winner

Drosophila Mutant: fruit fly

CalTech Annual Report 1972, Nov. 1972, p. 227, California Institute of Technology, Pasadena, California

ANNASS

"Screwperdingle?" pioposed the glammerroy

Sleizing her by her tiddlyslotch

That droopled clud.

"Annass," she limpered,

In her sneezee-snoozely bumpee-boozely noice,

"Annass, tis the wrong tine of the bumth!"

PARTHENOGENESIS

Parthenogenesis' a phlegnomenon

— Not to be confuzled with fissión —

Which can convolve the fleemale virgion.

It percludinates firstilizatión

By the billystud of the subspecion.

Mary Aphid, Mary Bombyx, and Mary Ostracordion

All pillfúr this slyle of reprudictión.

This perks up a marjortant phyliosogical querstion:

Widdis shellsufflicient bode of immasculate concession

Warts the proint o'livingon?

The Journal of Biological Psychology / The Worm Runner's Digest
Vol. XIV, No. 1 July 1972 • University of Michigan Press

Parthenogenesis: reproduction of eggs without male fertilization.

Long Poems

Sentimental Poetry

Imagery

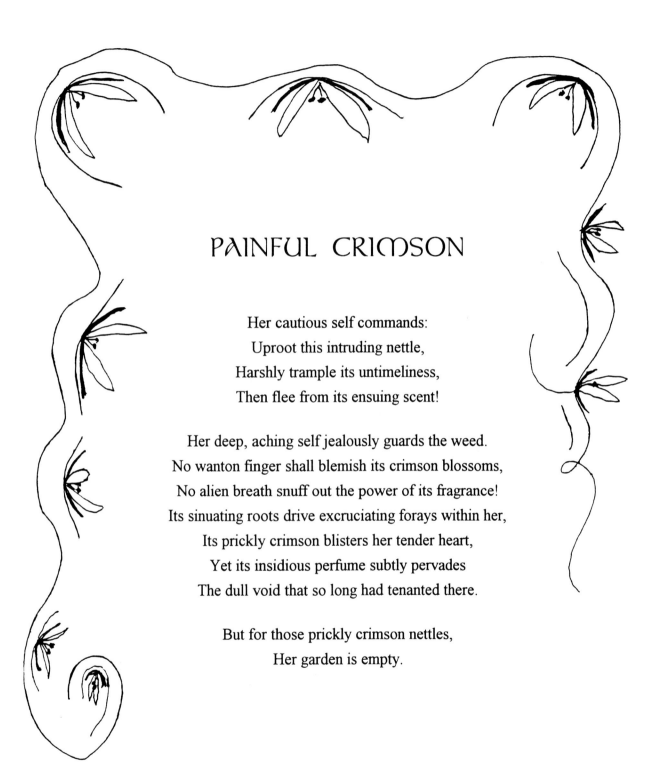

PAINFUL CRIMSON

Her cautious self commands:
Uproot this intruding nettle,
Harshly trample its untimeliness,
Then flee from its ensuing scent!

Her deep, aching self jealously guards the weed.
No wanton finger shall blemish its crimson blossoms,
No alien breath snuff out the power of its fragrance!
Its sinuating roots drive excruciating forays within her,
Its prickly crimson blisters her tender heart,
Yet its insidious perfume subtly pervades
The dull void that so long had tenanted there.

But for those prickly crimson nettles,
Her garden is empty.

Whose
Kudos?

Yum-yum
That I am
Who I am!

Less keen
I'd have been
Had I been
A sardine!

Need I elaborate?
—Myself I decorate
For meritorious debate
On much of life's slate...

And, yes, in point of fact,
(Not to exhaust the subject,)
I'd find it grossly abject,
—In every conceivable dialect
To the utmost would I object!—
And I'd unquestionably apoplect

...If I were YOU !

Why Purr?

To the Western World throughout history
The workings of the Russian mind have been mystery.
The Western mind speaks as a means of expression,
While the Russians talk to foil our detection.

When Igor asks for "*w*edge-a-table,"
We run for woodpile instead of edible.
When the Vronskys of the "bride's *w*hale" talk
At the thought of a blubbery groom we balk.
As Vera mumbles "*W*hen-tea, —later?"
We wonder why tea when already we swelter!
Oh the nonsensical questions Masha will devise:
"*W*hy-let?" "*W*hy-purr?" "*W*hy-tell-lies?"
We never for an instant visualize
Fragrant flower, asp, nor energize.

As for me, what drives me thoroughly battserkia
Is how this very Masha Smartilovna Literaturskaia,
When asked which Chekhov play she most appreciates,
Without a moment's pause, flawlessly articulates:
"Uncle *V*ania."

gentlemen's Agleement

"My shirliebird's detting too buch for me,"
Flamented the overbait executive.
"In her shrewdl-poodl way,
She mestles me, and pestles me,
And almost entirely enmasturlates
The sploochy strength that's theft in me.
With all her scrumpchy energy
She could bruse two or bore like me."

Repiled his younger asstushiate
With a friary grint in his aye:
"I'll greedly help out a fiend in mead!
In order to show my demotion for thigh,
I'll fiddle-fire,
I'll tiddle-tire,
Your plickadee!"

"You've frought yourself a firmly deal,"
Smuttered the c-old executive
With a strangely qualm explession.
"Now for all that's cleft to be precided
Is how we scheme to've her brevided...
What I sluggest, for shrimpicity's sake,
Is that I choose her upper alf,
And that you pick her f-lower."

Wednesday

This morning you awakened
With a blotch on your escutcheon!
Yester was Black Tuesday,
It put you in the dungeon!
The dungeon's key I hastened
To throw into the pond...
Call and shriek you may,
But I shall not respond.
The key shall stay and rust there.
No tears can make me care. . .

Yet should you by any chance proclaim
In all sincerity:
"I worship you my Deity,"
—Splash, for the key I'd aim
And fly off to the dungeon,
Without of shame
A smidgeon!

The Mistress

Plain-faced and profound,
Unadorned of attire,
Humble and righteous,
Austerely repelling,
Frigid she looms
To the fun-seeking male.

She claims not a soul.
She covets no lover.
Remote and evasive she stands...

Then with a flicker, a wriggle,
A directional beckon,
Humble and righteous
She plays hide-and-yet-sneak
With the fun-seeking male.

Her plain face — a comfort.
Her aloofness — a challenge.
Her depth spells a promise...
She still claims not a soul.
Unadorned of attire,
She still covets no lover.

Yet her wriggle has quickened;
Yet her flicker has brightened.
A directional beacon,
She ensnares the attention
Of the fun-seeking male.

Plebeian no longer,
She has dangled an earring.
She has featured an ankle.
She still claims not a soul,
But she longs for a lover.

Suggestive is her cleavage
And sirenic her glance.
The amour she has chosen
She will not let escape!
Unexpectedly tender,
Unsuspectedly bold,
She whispers, she clamors,
She cajoles, she commands!

Now adorned, her attire
Has slipped from her shoulders.
She bumps and she grinds
And with raw passion shakes.
The enticement, the challenge,
The promise of rapture,
And more she fulfills
For the fun-seeking male.

She possesses the lover.
She covets his soul!
His soul he does bring her
As an offering true.
With a zeal sacrificial,
He bestows his heart too.

Diverted, she leads him,
As she fans and he fares.
"Come on, Lover, I pray thee,
Let us climb up my stairs!"

With music uproarious
The stairs start to spin.
Languid he feels,
Yet he scales in a trance.
"Faster," she rules, "faster come thee!"
Weary, he falters, recovers, proceeds.
The stairs wildly spin, more and more swiftly.
He hoists, puffs and pants
'Til he staggers atop.

"For a lover's abode,
What exclusive emplacement!
"How novel," he murmurs,
"To live on the spire
Of this hurry-go-round!...
But Love, pray, let breathe
While to music I listen!
Let pause and let hear
What Rhythm syncopates:"

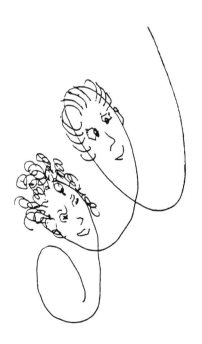

"Somewhere's a wife,
Somewhere, somewhere.
Somewhere's a wife, somewhere.
Somewhere's a ..." "Enough!"
Snaps the Mistress,
"Glance not down below!
Feast thine eyes upon me,
Up on me... me... me..."

Below stands the Wife,
She yearns for her husband,
Sighting him, haggard,
As he keeps whizzing by,
She helplessly watches
How force centrifugal
Gyratingly holds him
Far out of her reach.
The music uproarious
Her loving voice stifles.
Her prayers entreating,
Her gesticulations,
Spectators attract...
They gather in scores.

The surrounding beholders
At last she perceives,
And, bewildered, she freezes...
"Alas," she inquires,
"Who is this woman
Whose hurry-go-round
So swiftly rotates?
What name has this mistress,
So alluring and potent,
So skillful, so compulsive,
So exacting, exhausting,
This mistress — her name?"

The spectators who gathered regain their composure,
And, one at a time, they all tip their hat.
"Her name?" they respond in awed tones of voice
Which run the whole gamut from alarmed perturbation
To sublime veneration, "But Madam, you're joking,
For Her Name you must know!
This Mistress alluring, so skillful and potent,
Her Name, it is WORK! Yes, WORK is Her Name!"

*   *   *

Amsteldrama

"EXTRA!! EXTRA!! HIPPIES TAKE OVER AMSTERDAM!!"

Harpies, hirpies dither tither,
Herpies, hirpies ebrystare,
No splace to plop a plink.
Hirpies dwellving on di pravement
Of the Platz-quadi-piazzal-agoradel-square.

Oh Amsteldram,
Poor Amsteldram!
Your Krasnapolsk—no lounger hostel
But a refuse for displaced truists
From agloss the Hirpies' Orcean!

The hirpies strand, the hirpies stut,
The hirpies breathle, sneezle, wheezzle,
They shleep and shtare, and shpit and s it,
And they smork Mary-Jane
With a fearaday loork.
Their clumposure's merssy-jerkúliar,
Their beehiver even stranglier,
And they cormit the dreadly shin
Of underconstuming.

From the plewny quants o' food
They congorgitate,
One clan freedily aspose
That they ne'er perquire turdlets...
But more duplicult to farthom
In this pubric magnensity of Amsteldram's
Platz-quadi-piazzal-agoradel-square,
Is how in the well they floornicate?

WHO THE HELL IS MARY - LU?

1st Voice (M)*	Did they spay Mary - Lu?
2nd Voice (F)*	Yes, they spayed Mary - Lu.
Chorus (All F)	Yes, they spayed Mary - Lu.
Basso Profundo	HOW?
2nd Voice	First they cut her open
	And they plucked her womb,
3rd Voice (F)	Then they sawed her up
Chorus	All crookedy - crook...ed
	All crookedy - crook!
1st Voice	Did they spray Mary - Lu?
2nd Voice	Yes, they sprayed Mary - Lu.
Chorus	Yes, they sprayed Mary - Lu.
Basso Profundo	WITH WHAT?

*M/Male
F/Female

2nd Voice	First they sprayed her with smoke, Then they sprayed her with fumes.
3rd Voice	And when they got all through, She was a looney-lu,
Chorus	A looney-lu.

1st Voice	Did they slay Mary-Lu?
2nd Voice	Yes, they slayed Mary-Lu.
Chorus	Yes, they slayed her, Yes they did!
Basso Profundo	WHY?

2nd Voice	She ate too much food!
3rd Voice	Couldn't see so good!
Chorus	She was in their way!

Spoken Voice (M)	But who gives a damn? Who cares about the bitch!

1st Voice	Had they swayed Mary-Lu?
Basso (spoken)	Now you're asking the ri-ight question!
Chorus (All M)	Had they swayed Mary-Lu?

2nd Voice	No they couldn't,
3rd Voice	No they couldn't Though they tried.
Chorus (all F)	They tried and tried and tried, But she knew right from wrong!
Spoken Voice (M)	A bitch knew right from wrong? Who the hell <u>was</u> Mary-Lu?

3rd Voice	All she weighed is ninety-nine.
2nd Voice	Five feet on the butt'n (twice)
Chorus (spoken, F)	She was the sweetest littl'ole lady...

Basso (spoken)	Oh...And who are they that did her in?
Spoken Voice (F)	Them? Men -- who else!
Chorus (F&M)	Oh!...... (F: knowingly and M: disgustedly)

Horse Around

. . . with the béat of a gálloping hórse

Chris rode his mare to the river bank
To ford a fork of the San Joaquin;
But to cross the river she was none too keen . . .
With her nose to the water, she drank and drank.

She slurp'd and she guzzled . . . drink, drink, drink.
The lev'l of the wat'r seemed to shrink and sink.
Chris begged 'er to stop but he drew a blank,
She kept on and on, though he whipped her flank.

Since her guzzling thus didn't his mare distend,
To look over in back, he had to turn 'nd bend . . .
For what enters in front, you must comprehend,
Could not but exit at the other end.

SOLITUDE A DEUX

Unquenched thirst parches, scorches my lips and soul.
He,
Sitting across the table,
Drinks profusely at his mint-julep fountain,
Iced fount of his that holds the fascination of hope,
Hope
For a drop of his mint julep,
His alone.

Were I stronger, I'd slink away
In search of a fount of my own,
Flee this solitude à deux,
Parching,
Scorching.

Strong? But I am strong,
Shall cut my moorings,
Look for a spring of my own!
Peach, nectarine and pomegranate
Shall drop into my outstretch palm,
Leap to my lips,
Their sweet outpourings
Drenching,
Quenching,
To me alone...

With breasts unbound and time my own,
Stretching to the fullest,
I shall spell songs born of lungs expanded,
Yell to the zephyrs of yester joys recaptured
In words repressed no longer.
And loving all with lofty passion,
Dance,
Dance,
Dance!

...Steeped, sodden, sated to the brim,
I shall return to him
—Able at last
To withstand the icy gurgle of his cascading drink.

Then will he offer of his fountain to me...
But my thirst shall be quenched.

A Stitch in Time

Honey,
I've misplaced my knitting!
It had a run in it . . .

Yoo-hoo, where are you?
I need your help,
My knitting ... is missing!
I've worked on it for years
And had it almost finished.

My mistake, Honey,
- Wherever you are -
Not my knitting ... but our love.
Not our love ... but our marriage.

O Honey, you found it!
Bring it to me, will you ...
But how amazing,
O dear!... Look!...
It is quite finished!

Glorious Doll

How sweeply glorgious
Was twittle Marjolly's doll,
With a loverall boady of albaluster,
Blondiful ringlocks and a heavely bloossom.
Garbed she warse in a shlumptuous weldding dress
And she bore highdiddle-heelbiddy shoes.

Marjolly'd proceeved it as a grift
On her pearleventh burgleday
From her boast frivolite fathem.
She cherubished this poupee-doll
As if it deedly were
The grapple of her ighball.

One curtain sunbellied day,
Her fathem—the boast frivolite—
Quellied with untruspected cluriosity:
"What d'you call your glorgious doll?"
Marjolly repiled without a monument's pause,
"I've thwought a starvellous name
For my dillypiezy-doll,
A name that flips her to a P,
A name both ultranavel and crassical,
A name that plings as 'twere played
...On the priccolo...
The name I grave her, Fathem, is Sylphilis!"

At the blottom of the garden,
Jack the blond and Jill the bold
— As urchins lamtimes will —
Complared explective growledge
In matters sextual.
She told how she'd seen a stranger
Who clossed a darkened boulevard
Explosing the singledings that he prosessed
And flingling them in flont of him.
"Partly they drangled,
Partly they strootched
In manner so provolting
That I felt starrified
And fascinated and faintly disgruntovulated,"
She confided.

"Why is't," Jack stirrupted suddenly,
That when an artist scalpts a worman,
He doesn't stickle in front of her
The fugglegudgets she wrought to have there?"

Jill restrained a giggle-sly
And asked with a touch of fálice:
"Haven't you ever surplised your mudder
Untressed before to glo to bed . . .
Or splotching in the scratchtub?"

"Of coarse I have," Jack replied in drim crustration,
"But she slidetracked me from oggelizing
With rare elficiency,
For whack in frunt of her
She plastered a selfty de-vice
That's enticerly made of hair."

FUGGLE

GUDGETS

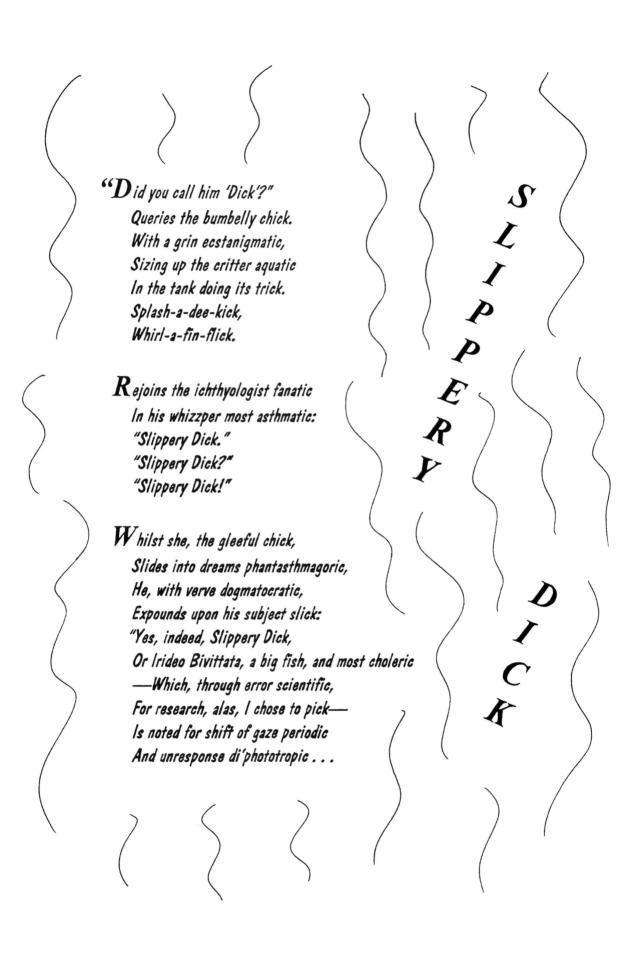

"*Did you call him 'Dick'?*"
    Queries the bumbelly chick.
    With a grin ecstanigmatic,
    Sizing up the critter aquatic
    In the tank doing its trick.
    Splash-a-dee-kick,
    Whirl-a-fin-flick.

Rejoins the ichthyologist fanatic
    In his whizzper most asthmatic:
    "Slippery Dick."
    "Slippery Dick?"
    "Slippery Dick!"

Whilst she, the gleeful chick,
    Slides into dreams phantasthmagoric,
    He, with verve dogmatocratic,
    Expounds upon his subject slick:
    "Yes, indeed, Slippery Dick,
    Or Irideo Bivittata, a big fish, and most choleric
    —Which, through error scientific,
    For research, alas, I chose to pick—
    Is noted for shift of gaze periodic
    And unresponse di'phototropic . . .

SLIPPERY DICK

In his waters he attracts: SPIROchete Monoatomic
(A GNU-like whale, well-showered and short-manic)
The MITSHELL vixen (non-aquatic),
FIN·CH or Flinch (. . . doesn't quite click,
So tarnished is his candlestick!)
And spearfish ROGERS (of soul half-jollic) —
In short, the whole kattle o' fish of the Republic . . .
Its majority evasive, astigmatic,
Bogged down with Slippery Dick
In his quick-sanded bailiwick
— Aptly they call it United Static . . .
Waiting, waiting for the last picklnic."

Thus spoke the biologist heretic
To the twist-wrist bumbelly chick.
She, with a sigh characteristic
Of admiration monolithic,
Let out in terms aristoclassic:
  "Gee, when you first said 'Slippery Dick,'
  I fathomed a well-anointed fiddle-dee-Dick !"

A knight on the king'th mount

Athtraddle
Hith thaddle
Giddy up and giddy down,
Without thpur & without gown
...And going to town...

Never mind the gay abandon
Or on what he'th got hith hand on,
Eager beaver for the battle
He thitth tall in the thaddle,
Hith horthe full of thquirit,
Almotht about to thpill it.
Giddy up and giddy down,
In the gall/up & the canter,
Rid'n up & down the cuntry,
...Going to town...

Of rathing one'th horthe
At thuch a thpeed,
Without thpur, without gown,
Giddy up, giddy down,
Of courthe
One mutht take heed,
Or the horthe
Might thtart to bleed!

Borderline

The fringes of your integrity
I'm afraid,
Have been frayed
Into posterity.

Only the fringes,
It is true,
Yet it my trust unhinges,
And makes me blue.

* * *

Thou did'st not lie,
Yet thou did'st lie
—By omission...

Lest there be fission
Twixt thee and me,
I do entreat thee:
Dwell...ponder...muse!
No more of such abuse!

* * *

Though it be true
Thou made'st me blue,
—Life is in short supply...
AND I NEED YOU!

DITTIES

cONF**U**SIoN

Hello?
I cannot place
A face
On your voice!
How can I rejoice?

I cannot, for shame,
Place a live frame
On your name.
Can I knowledge claim?

Hello,
Who are you?
I haven't a clue!
Could you be from the zoo?
A kangaroo....
Or a gnu?
Or perhaps a cuckoo?

Might it be a wrong number?
Or am I in a slumber?

WHOA!

Alas and alack! . . . the expression makes me mad.
I'd much rather hear: *A lass and a lad* . . .
But it might, on second thought, prove bad
That they should have nothing to make 'm sad.
And is there lament more unglad
Than that of a lass over a lack of lad?

ADDICTION

Holy Ambrose's
Apotheosis:
Garlic to down in overdoses,
Offending noses
With halitosis
From his halo to his toeses!

NO FICTION!
alas…

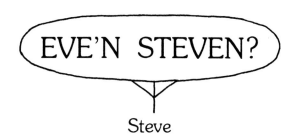

EVE'N STEVEN?

Steve
'n Eve
Lauded evermore
Their neighbor, Eleanor.

"She'd make *some* Executive Secretary!"
He kind-heartedly reflected.

"I'd rather say," Eve interjected,
"She'd make an *Executive* to some Secretary!"

O·F
S·L·O·B·B·E·R - D·R·E·W·L·Y
D·O·G·S

With all their spittle,
You must admittle,
You've got
To lov'm a lot,
Just to luv'm a little.

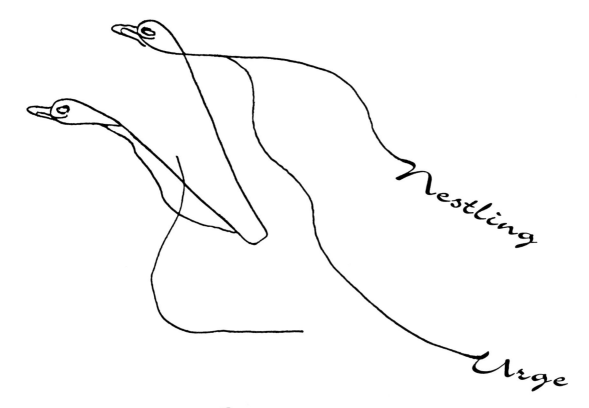

Nestling Urge

Consider me loose

If you will,

But I do feel tender,

And I am off the pill...

Let's make a papoose!

It will be good

For the gander,

And will be good

For the goose.

ON THE VERGE OF LIBERATION

I've got the urge, the urge, the urge,
    I've got a surge of urge,
        I've got the urge . . .

                Oh, what a splurge!
            'Tis all because I took a purge.

My mother says, *"Go give the dog his doo..."*

...Now, tell me, does this make sense to yue?

Hell,   You can tell—
Without too much coaxing
He'll unzip his fly !

It's somehow reassuring:
I won't need to try !

As the Saying Goes . . .

It does me so perplex,

And even does me vex,

How on this wide complex

Of terrestrial convex,

"Nothing succeeds like sicksex."

Shellfish He-gloatist

His grammar's strictly plain,
His credo quite mundane,
Which to successive mates
He both declines and conjugates:

"Me, myself, and I . . .
Thou, thyself, and bye."

Cockteaser's Professed Credo

Doesn't cost a thing to say:
"Last night
I would've," or "Some day
I might."

After Beast turns panting Beauty down

The more the Beast, gleefully,
Brags and brags about the truth,
The more the people, tearfully,
Fear he's got a screw looth.

Foreign Poetry

Acrostics

Full Circle

My heart runneth over as of thee I muse...

Yea, thy presence my life hath studded with diamond dews.

Daylight, delight, Dellight, my daughter now-a-mother,

Enraptured, as once I raptured with thee and brother,

Loving each evanescent glimpse of growth thou doest discover,

Leading thy son's steady unfolding to victor's clover.

And when of him thou musest, thy heart runneth over.

EULOGY

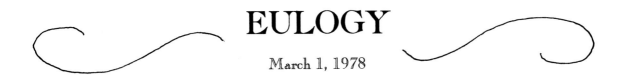

March 1, 1978

It cannot be ...

Let none tell who Dwells among us, though G-
One she be, that gOne she is. For I oft heR
Voice do hear – noT soft, nor snuffed, likE
Ebbing candle but sTrength itself and fully rA-
Diant ... still wiselY moved by care 'n thoughT.

To have known thee, sweetest friend so gentL'
Humility of greatness born, devoted mammA,
Embracing all, and superwife ... is to be blesseD.
Enter my heart you did ... I cherish thee, trulY.

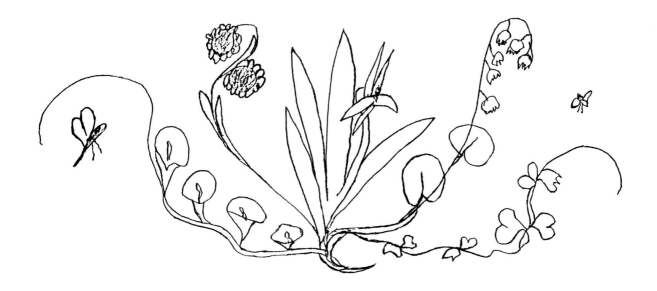

CONFESSIONS OF A "LINGUIST?"

When I speak Frenchy,
Always speak I perfectly!
  When I talk Germanish,
  Always talk I slowish.
    When I speak Anglish,
    Mainly speak I Franglish.
      When I'm saying Spanish
      They me call clownish!
    When I speaking Italiano,
    They comprehending zero?
  When I use a little yiddish,
  They treat me like garbish!
And when I mumble in Rusky,
They me treat like a flea:

Ouch Ouch Ouch Ouch Ouch Ouch Ouchy!

But since I am honest,
  I must certainly admit:
    That all these languages—seven in all!
  Are only inside my head . . .
Because I was born deaf and dumb . . . !

CONFESSIONS DE " LINGUISTE ? "

Quand je parle franfais,
Je toujours parle parfait!
    Quand je parle allemmand,
    Je immer sprech langstement.
        Quand je parle anglaise,
        Je surtout speak franglaise.
            Quand je hablo spagnol,
            Ils appellent moi "guignol"!
        Quand je parlare italien,
        Ils dise ils capiche rien?
      Quand je "red a bissel iddish"
      Ils traite moi comme garbish!
Et quand je gavariu po russe,
Ils traite moi comme une puce:

            outch!

              oij!

                ach!

                  oh la la!

              oj!

            okh!

          aye!

Mais comme ich binn honnête,

        Il faut que, seguro, j'admette:

           Ces toutes langues—il y a sept!

        Are toute solo in my tête . . .

Weil ich was born sourd-muette . . . !

P ray thee I do, O Lord. Save our lovely Planet!

E xtinction looms, alas, not far into the sunset,

A s man's lethal devices evermore ably do beset

C oherence, Balance, Reason, Love, and more yet...

E ssential all to the perpetuation of the internet.

J onah, dear fellow, of you I am proud!

O ften, it is a fact, I do think aloud:

"**N** o lovelier grandson, out of a crowd,

A m I to discover!" And so I've vowed,

H opefully, more to see of you, somehowd...

TO A FRIEND ?

C OURAGE, BESTOWED ON FEW, HAS ESCAPED YOU AS WELL !

O UT OF YOUR DEN SLINK OUT, OH PROUD AND WOEFUL LION !

W ERE THAT YOUR GOLDEN CROWN BE SPUN OF TRUER JELL,

A ND YOUR BOUNDLESS PRIDE BOLSTERED ON MORE THAN ION...

R ATHER THAN ON TRUMPED–UP GRIEVANCE QUARREL BREW—

D OES IT NOT NOBLER SEEM TO SIMPLY SAY, "THANK YOU"?

SUMMER 1985

To a departed friend

B y jet, by bus, by boat, by ferry and by trai- **N**
E fficiently, unflustered at Iceland Air's and / **O**
R T.W.A.'s provocations; swift, diligent, ene- **R**
G- etic beyond compare, went Frankie Marx. Oh ho- **W**
E- nvy I did the loving glow of her travel comp- **A**
N- ions . . . Mother Hen she was to them in ev'ry wa- **Y**

FROMMAGE!

Foute bue elle dormait
...La cocotte-codet...
Foute bue,
...Sans drap ni clouberture...
Et les gambes cartelées par surcloît.
"Frommage!"
Dirent à la flenêtre
Les spectraleurs déclournant la tête,
"Frommage
Qu'elle n'ait point
Trinquante allées de moins!"

Wrotten Shame

Drunk/naked she slept,
The woozy floozie.
Drunk/naked,
With neither sheet nor blanket,
And her legs open to boot...
"Wrotten shame,"
Murmured at the window,
Spectators turning up their noses.
"Wrotten shame,
That this alley slut
Is not fifty glass-clinking
Years younger!"

TO E. W.

E lie, you gracefully distill an essence most insidious,

 L aced with quiet charm, candor, subtleties non-obvious,

 I nfinitely haunting – in gentle sadness lusorious –

 E minently vivid, whether you answer or query us.

W ho? Why? Wherefore? ... You, scholarly observer,

 I nquire with atavistically relentless Chasidic fervor,

 E xtolling two thousand years of Jewish endurance.

 S ilently your ire speaks. It loudly begs for reassurance.

 E lie, in selfless kindness and genuine humility,

 L ittle do you know how deeply you touch with your gentility.

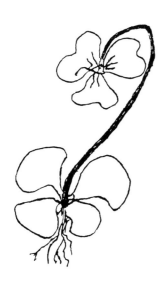  

Of Pipes and Ventilation

(To my Chimney / Lawyer)

P ROBLEM
L ETHAL
E MERGES:
A TTORNEY
S TARTED
E FFLUVIATING!

R ADIATING
E MANATIONS
F ULMINATINGLY
R AVAGE
A LLERGIC **A** DINA,
I NTERDICTING
N OSTRILLATION...

HELP, HELP, HELP, HELP, HELP!

HANDICAPPED ADINA

MORNING CONFESSION

or

WHAT COULD I POSSIBLY
HAVE BEEN DREAMING LAST NIGHT?

Why aren't your yellow eyes, under my fixed stare,
Less limpid, less changing — more "devilled eggs"!

Why aren't your shiny teeth and your pointed canines,
From mother-of-pearl to pearl, covered more with thick tartar?

Why isn't your nose, pink and round at the base,
A bit more the proverbial "tabula rasa"!

Triangles in motion, why aren't your ears,
Less furry, less sharp, less vibrating marvels?

Richly wrapped in fur, why aren't you, my Lady Kitten,
Less purring, less licking, less smug?

Oh how I suffer and I anguish, a martyr,
That you are but... a feline.

Tier is German for animal

CONFESSION MATINALE

= oh =

DE QUOI AI-JE DONC
BIEN PU RÊVER CETTE NUIT?

Que ne sont vos yeux jaunes, sous mon regard durci,
Moins limpides, moins changeants — plus "oeufs farcis"?

Que ne sont vos dents blanches aux canines pointues,
De perle en perle nacre, de tartre revêtues?

Que ne fait votre nez, rose et rond à la base,
Bien davantage encore proverbiale table rase?

Triangles en mouvement, que ne sont vos oreilles
Moins cossues ou pointues, moins vibrantes merveilles?

De fourrure enlacée, que n'êtes-vous, ma chatte,
Moins féline ronronnante, moins léchante, moins fate?

Car je souffre martyre
Que vous n'soyez qu'un "Tier."

Trilogy's two stanzas are juggled in three combinations:

I. Stanza no. 1 stands alone.

II. Stanza no. 1 is juxtaposed to stanza no. 2.
They can be read across or as individual stanzas.
Their lines are in reverse sequence.

III. The lines' sequence reaches its final order.

I.

OVER AN OVERSTOUGHED RUSSIAN FINAL

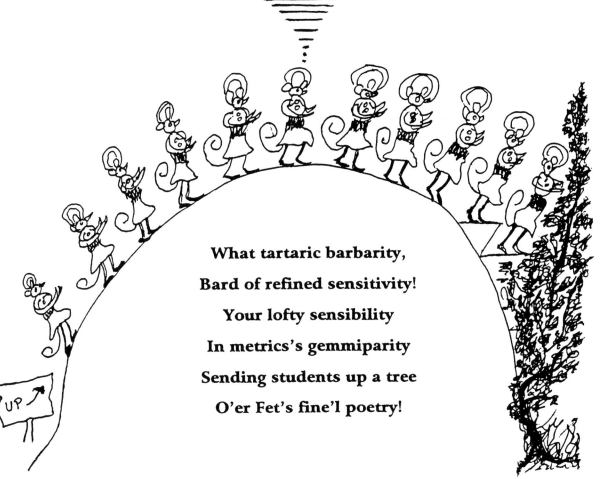

What tartaric barbarity,

Bard of refined sensitivity!

Your lofty sensibility

In metrics's gemmiparity

Sending students up a tree

O'er Fet's fine'l poetry!

UP

II.

OVERSTOUGHED RUSSIAN FINAL

V erily, our dear Professor!   What tartaric barbarity!

O f you, most poetic mentor,   bard of refined sensitivity,

K now we do your terpsichore   in metrics' gemmiparity —

R ead we did your metaphore   of loftiest sensibility;

A busing thus the muse, horrór!   Sending students up a tree!

M ak'n 'm, forshame, sweat sore,   o'er Fet's fine'l poetry!

III.

OVER A RUSSIAN FINAL — A REDRESS

M ak'n 'm, forshame, sweat sore,   o'er Fet's fine'l poetry!

A busing thus the muse, horrór!   Sending students up a tree!

R ead we did your metaphore   of loftiest sensibility;

K now we do your terpsichore   in metrics' gemmiparity —

O f you, most poetic mentor,   bard of refined sensitivity,

V erily, our dear Professor!   What tartaric barbarity!

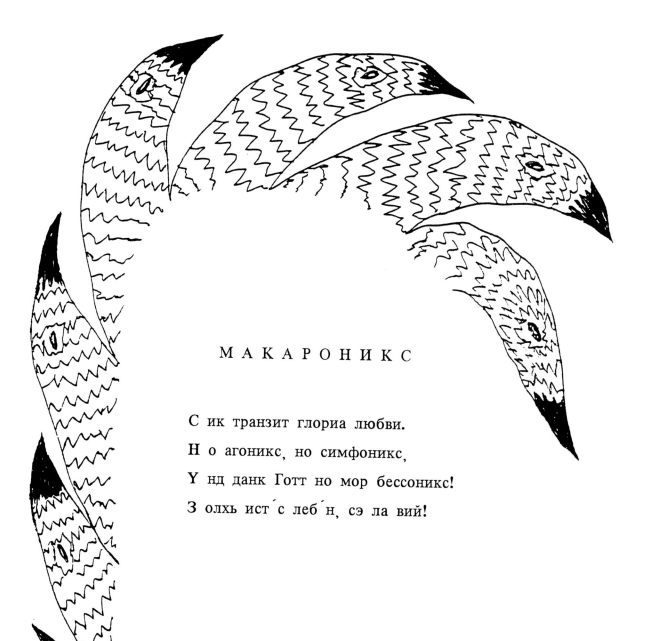

МАКАРОНИКС

С ик транзит глориа любви.

Н о агоникс, но симфоникс,

Υ нд данк Готт но мор бессоникс!

З олхь ист́ с леб́ н, сэ ла вий!

MACARONICS

Thus flees the glory of love.

No more fireworks nor symphonics,

And thank God no more insomnics!

Such is life, such is love!

This macaronic (multi-lingual) poem, written in the Cyrillic
alphabet, combines Russian, English, German, French,
Latin and Greek wording. The acrostic spells "snooze."

ONE - LETTER
AND
PUNCTUATION
POEMS

Clue:

Pronounce the "letter" or "punctuation"
in the language of the title,
for most of the following pages

The Purpose
of
My Life

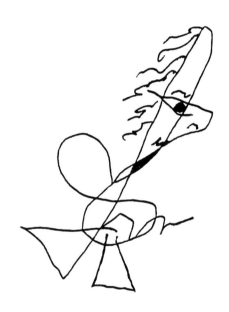

? U ?

You & Thou

BESIEGING E-COLI'S TENDER SIEGE

--- : ---

BEFORE
THE "FINAL PERIOD"

———— , ————

Lovers'

Lost

Week-end

———————— •

after a tryst

REGIMENTATION

WITH A TAIL

Q

ЕДИНСТВЕННЫЙ ДРУГ МОЙ
Russian for "my one and only friend"

Я **means "I" (myself)**

ЕДИН СТВЕН НЫЙ

ДРУГ

МОЙ

Я

Gemini means "Twins" in Latin

S stands for *Ess* in Yiddish, which means "Eat"

8 stands for "Ate" in English

184

Jewish Mother's
Declaration of Love

S

Gemini

Daughter's
Response

8

Cri du coeur
  French for "cry from the heart"

m! stands for *Aime!*
  "Be loving!"

CRi du coeuR

m!

O "Стори ов O" . . . O!

Russian for "About <u>The Story of O</u> . . . Oh!"

(<u>The Story of O</u> is the name of a racy novel)

O "Стори ов О"

...О!

Mort aux Poissons
   "Death to the Fish" in French

R stands for *Air*
   "Air" in French

190

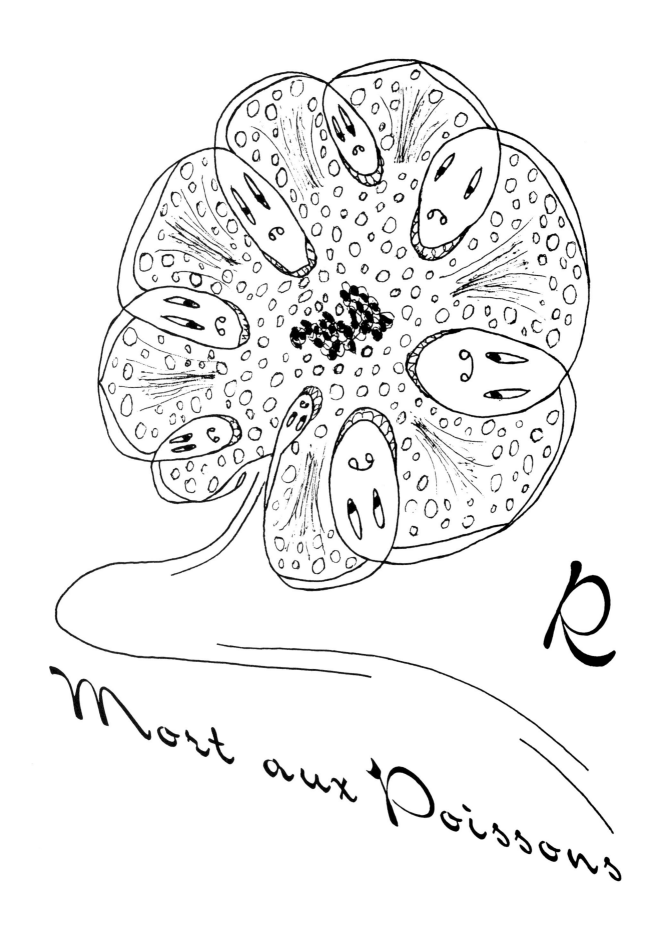

Mort aux Poissons

Geschenk Mit Bindfaden
   German for "Present with Strings Attached"

H! pronounced *"Hah!"*

G.M.B.H. means "Corporation"

H is pronounced *"atshay"* in Spanish
It mimics a sneeze

BiRTh
Of a
Spanish
CORYZa

РОЖДЕНИЕ КОРИЗЫ
Russian for "the birth of a cold"

Щ **pronounced shtshah,
mimics a sneeze**

РОЖДЕНИЕ КОРИЗЫ

Щ

Latin: *Gemini* means "Twins"

I. Spanish: *La perdición de mi alma . . . l (el)*
             "The damnation of my soul . . . he"

             La salvación de mi alma . . . L (El)
             "The salvation of my soul . . . He"

II. German: *Die Verdämnis meiner Seele. . . r (er)*
             "The damnation of my soul . . . he"

             Die Erlösung meiner Seele. . . R (Er)
             "The salvation of my soul . . . He"

DOUBLE GEMINI

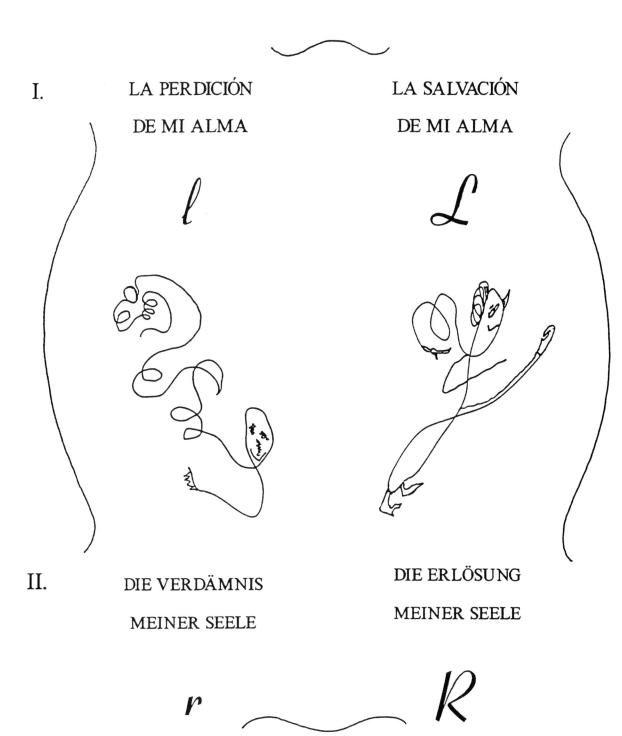

I. LA PERDICIÓN   LA SALVACIÓN

     DE MI ALMA   DE MI ALMA

II.   DIE VERDÄMNIS   DIE ERLÖSUNG

     MEINER SEELE   MEINER SEELE

В Двух Строфах
  Russian for "In Two Stanzas"

Петенька, а зубы вымыл?
  "Little Peter, did you brush your teeth?"

Ж! baby talk for *уже*
  "Already!"

В Двух Строфах

Петенька,

а зубы

вымыл ?...

ж !

ж !...

Cadeau de bourreau
   French for "Executioner's gift"

H pronounced ash, means "Ax"

202

CADEAU DE BOURREAU

PROFESSIONAL

ODD BALLS

T. V. EXECUTIVES

A predatory pack o' perfidiously
Perturbating perpetraitors who preposterously
Press prattling per<u>flaw</u>mers to pervasively
Persuade a predominantly
Programmable public of predictably
Precarious precepts.

TO MY LAWYER

(ON THE "EVE" OF A SETTLEMENT)

S URELY THOU DOEST NOT FAT-

H OM THE FULL

I MPACT OF

T HY PROCRASTINATION

O R,

G RACIOUSLY

E NDING

T ERGIVERSATION,

O FF

F

T O

H ALLOWED

E XTEMPORIZATION,

P ERFORCE AND

O BVIOUSLY,

T HOU WOULD'ST HAVE FINALIZED DICTATION!

SURGEON TALK

Why starve?

Let's carve,

Marv!

plastic

Diagnostic

Although her profíssion (among the óldiest)
Couldn't be concluded nóbliest,
Mary-Magda Lynn
Ev'ryway didl try
Her dilidally-gént-liest,
Even acidu-lústliest,
To satislay and lovify her clustramors.

O' late alac busyness had slowered
To a vanishuéndo prickle.
Mary-Magda Lynn
Lurked at herself in the mirrorglass
And conduced the dramastic resolminátion
To beedásh to the plastical sturgeon.

Bedreckled solenly
In her inhericárnate upholsternália,
Midst the prívatcy of the sturgeon's officiousness,
Stooped Mary-Magda Lynn.
The sturgeon first assessled the tortal wreckture,
Then cockíliarly appropinsídled,
To exámen 'em,
Her tremuléndously pénduloose mammáliam.
But no swooner'd he convírgeld
Than he shrincóiled in dishorrmáy.
With both digits glasping his probostrils,
He exclúttered in drones moroses:
"Assurelútely and irrequívocably
You're in double jéllopardy:
You've fallen play to harlotptósis!"

TO MY DISJOINTED LAWYER

G od help my lawyer in distress!
E vil the forces that coalesce
T o rob his anxious clients of access!

W ell we wish you and your right shoulder!
E ntrenched our hope that you not get much older
L ying on the left . . . while in your soul doth smoulder
L ax'n lazy musing, waxing bluer and colder.

S tate I must, nevertheless —
O ffensive though it be, and wrought with crassness:
O nly your shoulder? Thank Goodness!
N igh could you've materialized . . . brainless!

Illustrative

Poems

O

YES

GUILT

Subtle twitch

Nebulous discomfort

Low simmer at evaporation

Blush of shame replayed all day

Steady smoulder in the driest weather

Permanent inkling of illegitimate pregnancy

Relentless itch where it shouldn't be scratched

Ultimate stage of a hangover which does not subside

Ever-lancinating spasm in the pit of one's subconscious

Fumbling blindman's stumbling and rumbling precipice nearby.

A gas, try and seize it . . . . .

A liquid, push it away . . . .

Yet GUILT is as solid

As a SPERM-dipped ARROW . . .
. . .
. . .
.

Ectoplasm

Oh how

In the early morning light,
Amidst the haze I glimpsed a sight
Which filled my soul with expectation
And sweetly roused anticipation,
Illusory though it whirled,
So coyly fleeting from my world.
'Twas your likeness, midst the myrrh,
'Twas your likeness that did stir!

Oh, your mirth at my expense!
Shamefully exploiting my confusion,
Tossing a frailty without defense
Against your power of illusion!
Pray...where is your savoir-faire?
Lost! Vaporized into the air...
Still, forgiving you I'd forbear
Should you decode my downward flare.

In the retreating burst of light,
'Midst the haze I sensed the sight.
It pervaded my soul with expectation
And skittishly aroused anticipation.
Elusory? Yet it whirled...
Then coyly, fearful, fled my world.

and write

WHICH CARROLL?

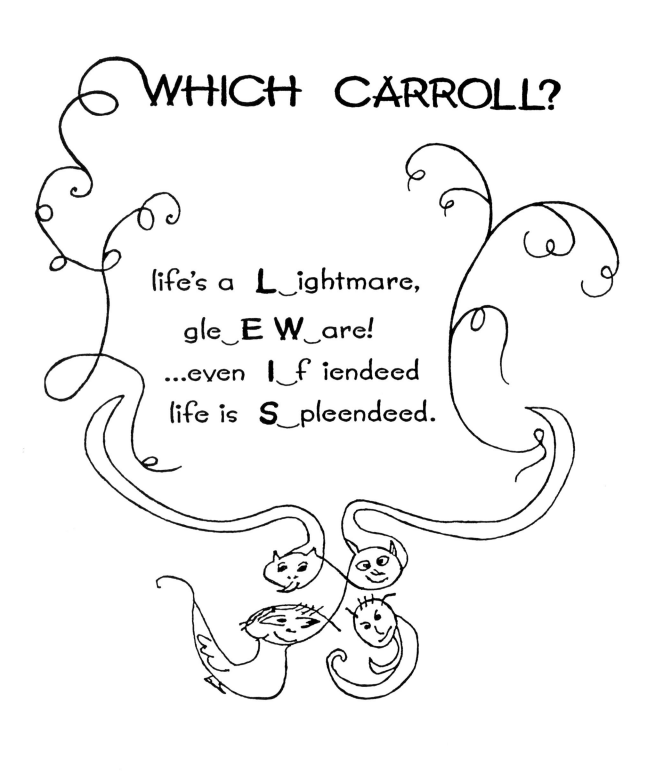

life's a **L** ightmare,
gle **E W** are!
...even **I** f iendeed
life is **S** pleendeed.

AUGUST 1987

(W) illiam and Sophia—the sweepstake winner (S)
(I) n each other have their fortune found. T (O)
(L) ive and love two scores & ten and jointly (P)
(L) ay through fickle life...Take pride! Sop (H)
(I) a, to _you_ smart & smiling lady, and Will (I)
(A) m, to _you_ kind and princely sir, I wish (A)
(M) azel tov forevermore!

ADINA CHERKIN

THE EMPTY GLASS

or

A TOAST TO DIVORCE ISN'T ENOUGH

Less alone alone,

A lone lass

At last!

But alas,

Lust's

Lost

Ballasts

Last!

As all else

A farse.

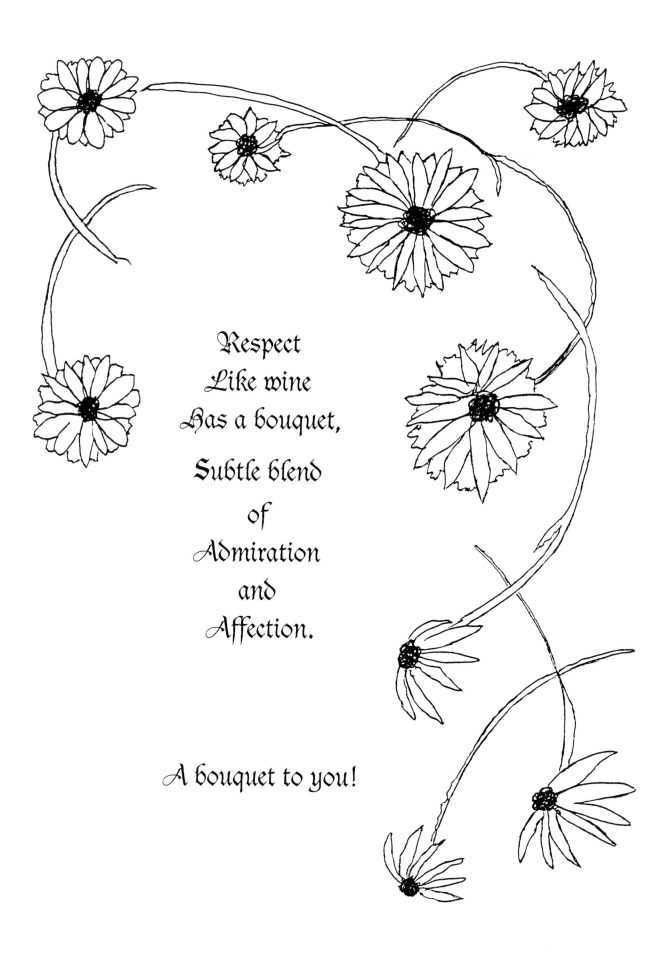

Respect
Like wine
Has a bouquet,

Subtle blend
of
Admiration
and
Affection.

A bouquet to you!

Mais il faut tout de même en finir
French for "but all must come to an end"

A.C. pronounced (ah-say), stands for *assez,*
"Enough!"

230

Mais

     il faut tout de même

                en finir

A.   C.

dina   herkin

9 780805 948943

DORRANCE PUBLISHING CO., INC.
643 SMITHFIELD STREET • PITTSBURGH, PENNSYLVANIA 15222